Sectarian Companies

Do you work in one of them?

Ismael Bello.

Dedication

To my family and all my friends for continuing to support
me in the projects.

Thanks.

To God for being a source of wisdom and understanding, for being my guide and my greatest truth.

To all colleagues and friends interested in this topic, which we always talked about until it materialized in this material.

To my wife Edith who has accompanied me in all my projects, this one in particular.

And above all to you dear reader for having acquired this book.

Index

Foreword.

Today there are many companies worldwide. Many of them are corporations or reputable companies that are well known for the great impact they have caused in society, whether at the international, national or local level.

Among the existing companies worldwide there are some so-called "Sectarian Companies" or "Labor Sects". These types of companies have been progressively increasing due to different factors, some of them are:

- They offer high incentives.

 - Offer high-cost courses and training.

 - Some make the schedule more flexible.

- They reward the achievement of objectives.

In this book you will know in detail what is a sectarian or sectarian enterprise, characteristics of this type of company, how to know if your company or the company where you work is sectarian or going towards that direction, what steps to take to change that situation or to out of it.

Read this book slowly, calmly, detail and analyze it, think if what is written here has something to do with you or someone you know. It is important to know that even if we do not find ourselves in a sectarian enterprise there are people we know who are or may be, and that is where we are going to influence them, to guide them and advise them and have an idea of where they are.

Thank you for purchasing this book and it will be of great help to you and many people.

ISMAEL BELLO.

Sectarian Companies   Ismael Bello

Chapter I.

Companies.

According to the Dictionary of the Royal Spanish Academy, the company is: "an organization dedicated to industrial, commercial or service activities for profit". It also indicates as a company "place where these activities are carried out".

With this pair of definitions we can say that the company as an institution, promotes the development of society through the activities it performs and as a work site, encourages the cognitive development of the individual.

Companies have been present since the industrial era, from that moment the company began to be a fundamental part of world development. And currently in the information age, companies continue to be a pillar in technological and industrial advances and developments.

It is enough to observe on television, on the internet, in the press or on city billboards, the large amount of publicity referring to companies or corporations of great renown, not to mention the companies that do not advertise, but that like those that do, are large companies, which due to their time in the market, are highly reputable.

Companies generate jobs, contribute to the Nation or State the respective taxes, encourage local production, create foundations and offer different products or services to solve local, national or international problems.

There are companies that generate confidence, because they have principles and do not deceive their employees, they learn and adapt to changes, the personal freedom of their employees is respected, communication is open and straightforward, they work in teams and, above all, take advantage of and develop the employee to be a possible entrepreneur, not a slave of the job.

I am in favor of promoting the company as a spearhead for the development of a community, city or country and for personal growth. What I am not a supporter of is that of companies that harm people through extreme commitments, punishing them without salary, without benefits or bonuses for an error committed, generating psycho-terror at work or making people dependent on work, with no option to freedom, because if they break the commitment with them they are cataloged as conspirators, enemies, fascists, revolutionaries and many other disconcerting qualifiers.

Of this type of companies we will speak in the next chapters, the companies called "Sectarian Companies" or "Labor Sects".

Chapter II.

The Sects.

In the previous chapter we read the definition of a company, we observe the advantages of companies and the contributions they make to the individual and society. At the end of the chapter we talked about sectarian or sectarian companies, but what are sects? We will define it below.

The term comes from the Latin seqüi: follow, and applied to schools of philosophy (where sectátor comes from and sectaries: 'adherent', 'follower'). The Dictionary of the Royal Academy defines it this way: "set of followers of a religious or ideological bias".

19

And also as: "religious or ideological doctrine that is differentiated and independent of another."

Note that the definitions have two keywords "follower" and "doctrine". Starting from these two words we will form the sect definition. Let us begin.

The only condition to be a follower of something or someone is that you like that something or someone without any commitment, that is, you always decide whether to follow it or not. On the other hand, when you follow someone or something through a doctrine it means that you have been educating, working or manipulating them so that you are a follower and this is what is called a sect.

You follow someone or something in most cases against their will, usually in the sects there is a leader or leaders who are the ones who give the rules, steps or rules so that people follow them to the letter and they indicate that you will obtain a benefit in the future, (another key feature of the sects is this), a future benefit, it is not an immediate benefit or in the now, that is, it is a promise offered, you do not even have a guarantee that what they offer will be given to them.

It is very common in sects to hear phrases like these: "you will obtain full freedom by following us", "you will have great advantages over others", "we are different", "every day we advance at the pace of victors", "to obtain results you must make an effort double "," every day we are more ".

The sects pursue the transformation of the personality of their followers to modify their interests, their values and their types of relationships. For this purpose, they use techniques of psychological manipulation, which are reflected in the different phases that the captured one lives.

Now let's see how there are companies that have indoctrination systems for their employees and how sectarian companies influence their employees.

Chapter III.

Sectarian Companies.

Sectarian companies, labor sects, business sects or commercial sects are companies that make the employee dependent on her through indoctrination or training, usually by offering a high salary package. It is indifferent if the company is sales or services. In addition to a high level of commitment that is exceeded in devotion.

Features.

Dave Arnott in his book "The Cult of the Company" points out: the three characteristics of a company sector: devotion, charismatic leader and separation from the community. Analyze these characteristics in detail.

1. Devotion: Devotion has to do with your loyalty or commitment to the company, organization or firm. You have to feel good about the company, or rather, you are the company, but only at the level of commitment. You have to sacrifice your free time if necessary so that the company stays and is up to date with all the activities that are committed.

2. Charismatic leader: The leader, the boss or the owner induce the employees to submission, generally, appealing to the positive emotions of the employee, but this is not always the case, there are

times when they resort to negative emotions, such as Fear or the insecurity, so that the employee feels unprotected.

3. Separation from the Community: This happens when the work returns to the life of the employee. The employee has at work; Nursery, bank, gym, sports courts, bookstore, laundry, medical service. And that's not all. The company gives: housing, walks, courses and other types of leisure and recreation activities, making us increasingly dependent on the company and away from the family and the community.

In this part it is important to point out in a timely manner the following aspects of a sectarian enterprise:

- The company adopts an aspect of religion.

- Employees isolate themselves from friends and family.

- Employees lose the perception of the world.

- Employees become fanatical and live out of reality.

- Employees lower their employability.

- The employees are increasingly dependent.

- The employees are exploited to the maximum.

- The company produces exit phobias.

- Employees who try to leave are criticized.

- The company creates espionage and surveillance agencies.

- The company applies psycho-terror to its employees.

- The company uses different methods of indoctrination.

- The company blames the employee for the error (s) he commits in the organization.

How do they work?

This question that you have just read I am quite sure that you did it before reading it, and that is why I am going to answer them at this moment.

The sectarian companies work basically in the same way, they use the system of recruitment, offering and retention.

1. Recruitment: To awaken the interest of the person or future employee, the company offers security and benefits, gives guarantees that it will solve their problems.

2. Offer: The person to be interested in employment or business, you begin to educate with typical languages of the institution. Once you enter the company, indoctrination begins with highly relevant offers, including personal growth, travel, power and money.

3. Retention: Then already within the company you will be introducing the person in a sense of fear and guilt so that it will be difficult for you to leave if you do not want to continue with them. He is branded as a traitor, conspirator, revolutionary, disloyal and enemy.

Causes to Enter a Sectarian Enterprise.

You may say, but if you know this about sectarian companies, why do people join them? As you will see, there are many reasons, the most important are the following.

- When they are young.

- When they separate from families.

- When industries change.

- When they leave a church or social group.

- When they divorce.

- When they do not find a job.

- When they are newly graduated.

- When they have no experience.

- When they want to increase their profits.

- When they do not find emotional support.

These are some reasons, but they are not the only ones, there may be other causes of greater weight for people to be part of business sects.

In addition to this I want to tell you about my personal experience, so that you can observe some of the characteristics mentioned here.

In the company that worked, they applied the system of "rewards - punishments". You were evaluated according to your performance, if you did not meet the minimum requirements, you did not receive a compensation bonus, you were considered to be working for another company, because according to your accounts, you could do what was entrusted and much more.

In addition, you entered the category that they called "minimum wage adjustment", this meant that the next time you made adjustment or wage increase you would only receive the minimum established, that is, if the increases or adjustments were between 5 and 25 %, I was only going to receive 5%, yes, as long as you were not part of the "dismissal due to force majeure" plan. If you were included in that plan, you were fired with four or five other people, for the simple fact of not fulfilling their expectations, which was generally, to work hard and after hours in order to comply with what was proposed, which It represented overwork for little gain.

Another interesting detail of this company was that you were "guarded", from your home to work, all your movements were calculated, you knew what you did in free time and weekends.

Another point to highlight is that they were "prohibited meetings or gatherings between colleagues", if you did they insulted him by telling him that the workplace was not for jokes, neither for union plans, nor for conspiracy.

Another characteristic of this company was that they produced "exit phobias", if you gave the impression of wanting to go they called you apart, they asked you about your situation, and they asked you questions like:

- What does he want?

- What are you going to do?

- Have you thought about your family?

- Do you need an increase or a bonus?

And if the answer you gave did not convince them, they would begin to threaten you:

- I work like this will not get?

- Nobody will pay what he asks for?

- This is where he was formed, and that's how he pays the company?

- Did this company believe in you, when nobody accepted it?

- Outside of the company will you be a simple person without direction?

And if this were not enough, they also said:

- Look what happened to Robert.

- Those who have left have tried to return.

- Those who left have no life of their own.

- Those who withdrew can not find employment.

- Those who leave can not return or talk to those who stay here.

To close, the most relevant feature was that they made it "dependent". They offered housing, a car and a motorcycle as part of the benefits. What did that represent? the following: you received the housing or the car or the motorcycle, but it was not yours, it was a loan, which meant that if you were fired you had to return the assigned, and also generated a condition, in case you were If you were to withdraw, you would be more difficult to leave because it would cost you to get rid of the goods that the company gave you, causing you a conflict between reality and the imaginary, they made you believe that you were the owner of what they assigned him, when in fact it was a simple loan.

Now at this point in my reading, I ask you, do the characteristics of a sectarian enterprise have something to do with your company or with the company where you work?

If your answer is negative, read on the next pages you may change your mind.

If your answer is affirmative, you are in an abyss, your personal life can be complicated if you do not correct certain patterns of behavior or if you do not change jobs, keep reading anyway, the next few pages will surprise you.

Chapter IV.

Identification of a Sectarian Enterprise.

You already read that they are companies, that they are sects, that they are sectarian companies or labor sects (their characteristics and how they work), now we will see how to identify a sectarian enterprise, how to know if one is in a sectarian enterprise or not.

The following data is unique to sectarian companies, be alert to these tips, so you will identify what situation you are in. Let us begin.

1. Announcement: The announcement is about the offer of employment or labor supply, it is important to emphasize that the announcement does not name the company anywhere, they do not mention the position they want to occupy, but they do mention what they offer and what kind of people seek. The ad is similar to this: "Company of Great Path, request: professionals or graduates in various areas with high desire to excel. The company offers: training within the company, high commissions, highly competitive salary package, unbeatable work environment ". Be alert to this type of announcement, it is possible that sometimes change the content of the notice maintaining the format.

2. Interview: After you have seen the announcement, you go and leave your curriculum summary, and call it that same day or the next to formally interview and

explain your employment in detail. It is there when you ask some questions similar to these:

a) Are you happy with your current job?

b) Are you comfortable with your current situation?

c) Would you be interested in changing your quality of life?

d) Would you invest a little time and money to earn a lot?

e) Would you like to be a person?

f) Would you like to work in a company that supports you and recognizes your merits?

g) Would you like to get everything you want?

h) Would you like to grow professionally?

Generally, this type of companies try to convince you to work in it, however, there are sectarian companies that look for qualified personnel in specific areas and do all kinds of tests, to know if you are reliable, honest and loyal.

3. Employment: When you are inside the company, what I call "psychological pressure" begins. This pressure can be in different ways:

a) Pressure to attend meetings, outings and visits of the company.

b) Pressure in your position or work area.

c) Insistence to attract more customers (If it is a product company).

d) Insistence that each day more effort to obtain more benefits (service companies).

e) Teaching or indoctrination through readings, videos and audios.

f) Use of an exclusive vocabulary of the company, usually call the person by title and surname (Engineer Smith).

g) Prize and punishments regime based on sales or service rendered.

h) You must treat your colleagues according to their position, friendships are forbidden.

i) Gatherings or group meetings are prohibited to deal with any topic.

j) Has one or more managers or supervisors who observe and analyze their performance.

k) Evaluations are done periodically through your superior to determine how much you deserve to earn.

l) The possibilities of promotion are minimal or they do it through the law of maximum effort.

m) The word "collaboration" is often used instead of "obligation."

n) You are prohibited from asking permission to study or take professional improvement courses outside of the company.

o) They monitor their personal and private life.

p) They make him dependent, offering him vehicles, trips or houses, so that later he finds it difficult to leave.

q) They make you feel guilty if the company has a discharge or a claim from a customer.

r) They ridicule you in front of your colleagues in case you do not want to follow the guidelines or rules.

s) If he tries to leave or decides to leave, they manipulate him and make him feel part of the family so that he discards that idea, and if he does not criticize him and try to damage his image.

t) They make him feel a high commitment to them, they treat him as if he were from the family.

u) They encourage obedience, affective commitment and irrational faith towards the leader or owner.

v) You find more satisfaction at work, than at home or anywhere else.

w) Your free time is getting smaller.

x) He can not have fun, have leisure time or entertainment, because he has to comply with the company.

Also note the phrases that these companies often say to their employees:

- "We are the leading company in the sector".

- "Our company has 300 million in stock" (or invoice 20 million daily).

- "We are present in everything (or almost everything) the country."

- "We are present on all continents and in more than 30 countries."

- "Our product (or our service) is a leader in the market".

- "We are the most awarded company in recent years".

- "You are an important person, because you are working for us".

- "Your social and economic status is (or will be) high if you stay here."

- "Your personal life has grown to count on us".

- "What will you do if you leave this company?"

- "You are the company and the company is you".

- "Everything you have you owe to this company."

- "If you leave the company you will lose power".

- "Nobody will hire you to know that you left here."

- "We need to see more results so that you get more benefits."

- "Be a leader not a friend".

- "You are an essential part of this company".

- "The company will not recognize you anything if you leave".

Remember that these are key phrases, phrases can vary, but keeping the same focus.

In my personal experience I have seen people who are trapped, they depend so much on the company, they do not have a life of their own, they allow themselves to be humiliated and accept what they give for the mere fact of not being evicted from the house they live in or of being fired. .

Others, as they do not know another trade, remain there without being able to do anything to change it. For me, it is sad and regrettable to see this kind of situation, they changed their freedom and their independence by being attached to a house; to a car or a job.

Now that you have more specific keys and specific points, I ask you.

Are you in a sectarian enterprise?

If your answer is negative, congratulations! you work or are in a company that values your personality and professionalism, respects your individuality and your freedom. But, in any case, keep reading, it will help you to be alert in case you change your company.

If your answer is positive, you urgently need to change company or make a change within the company to play in your favor, otherwise you will be extremely lost as a human and as a professional. I suggest you continue reading and observe the consequences of being in a sectarian or sectarian enterprise.

Sectarian Companies

Ismael Bello

Chapter V.

Consequences of Sectarian Companies.

We already observed in detail that it is a sectarian or sectarian enterprise, now we will know the consequences of this type of companies. Pay attention and take note of what is most relevant to you.

1. They generate in the employees fear, anguish, stress, anxiety and all kinds of psychological illnesses.

Remember that the body depends 90% of the brain, that is, everything that has to do with the neurological, psychological and motor system.

49

2. Generate physical exhaustion in employees.

In this case we are talking about the musculoskeletal system, remember that this type of companies make it work more, including weekends.

3. Generate in employees the loss of independence and freedom.

People become dependent on the company and not only that, they are monitored and know all their movements when they are not in the company.

4. Generate in the employees the loss of family and friends.

People leave family and friends aside because they have business time or extra time to earn more and are totally isolated.

5. They generate addictive behaviors in employees.

Among those that stand out: smoking, alcoholism and drug addiction.

6. They generate suicidal tendencies in people.

This is due to the large amount of pressure that has daily or consecutive and is intended as a means of exit.

7. Generate discomfort in personal relationships.

Mainly given by the bonus-punishment effect, if you are not up to the level or level required your relationships with others worsen.

8. They generate in the employees states of aggression and irritability.

When they do not feel comfortable with what they do or do not receive what they promised, they let off steam with this type of behavior.

9. They generate in the employees losses of the goals and projects.

The desire and enthusiasm are lost, people self-destruct and disinterested in future plans.

10. Generate an oversight of family responsibilities and commitments among employees.

They lose the notion of time and reality (They do not know what is real and what is imaginary).

11. They generate in the employees problems of affectivity and sexual desire.

They are left without affection and sexual activity because they are submerged in work.

12. They generate medical and psychological disorders in the relatives of employees.

Family members are affected by the behavior of the individual in the family environment.

13. They generate a higher probability of accidents for employees.

Either by neglect, negligence or instant carelessness.

14. They generate low productivity for the company.

Being under this regime, most of the employees look for escape routes, which produce a notable reduction in the direct benefits of the company.

15. They generate a hostile work environment for the company.

Every time there are more complaints and reports of harassment and physical and psychological abuse.

16. They generate an image of illegality to the company.

Companies taking courses or sectarian behaviors are immediately labeled as operating in illegality or have links with groups, individuals or criminal organizations.

These are just some consequences, sectarian companies in themselves, are harmful to the industry, to the community, to people and to countries.

At this moment I want to ask you, according to what you have read in this book, what do you think of the sectarian companies?

I would like to know your answer, for that reason, at the end of the book you will find my email addresses to find out your answer to this and all the questions asked here.

.

Chapter VI.

Keys to Leave a Sectarian Enterprise.

Until the previous chapter, everything related to sectarian companies or labor sects was discussed and it is possible that you have identified yourself with the characteristics, keys or points indicated.

In this part we will see, the recommendations to leave a sectarian business and the changes that should be made if you decide to stay in it.

But before entering the recommendations I would like you to answer "Yes" or "NO" to these questions:

- Do you feel happy or happy with your work?

- Do you feel peace and tranquility?

- Are you in good health?

- Do you learn at your job?

- Is it independent of the company?

- Did you grow or grow professionally?

- Do you have free time to enjoy with your family and friends?

If your answer is "YES", then you must decide what changes to make the most of the positive factors that the company offers, the important thing is that you do not lose your identity as an individual, keep the difference between work, family and community. If your answer is "NO", it is time to make significant changes in your life, it is likely that you do not have your own identity (your identity is the company where you are), you do not have time to enjoy, you have family problems, you do not have or he has few friends, is in debt, is depressed, has problems with his colleagues or his work group and worst of all (as I have said before) is dependent on the company, that is, lost the freedom that is the most important that the human being has after life.

Regardless of what your answers were, observe and analyze the following recommendations.

What to do if you are in a sectarian business or in a company that has that direction, but you like what you do?

In this case you have some options, which you can evaluate and take into account, remember that these keys or recommendations are not the only ones, but with them, you can have a clearer idea of how to face your problems, study what to improve and which of they apply.

1. Try as much as possible not to be so dependent on the company.

If you have a company house, hand it over and buy or rent one, if you have a car of them, hand it over and buy one or go to work in public transport, the idea is that you will be more and more independent.

2. Make work work in your favor.

Reserve time in your schedule for different activities, once or twice a week, and commit to them as you do with your work.

3. Be positive.

The most important thing for the body and for the soul is to be positive, positive thinking and having positivity in life makes the individual more efficient and productive in all areas.

4. Learn everything you can.

If it is the job that you like, do not miss the opportunity to learn everything that has to do with your field. Learn, but do not punish yourself by taking extra work.

5. Change the site.

During the lunch hour, you can go to a park, have lunch at a restaurant or simply go out for a drink.

6. Remember who is outside of work.

Important for your life. Do not lose the perception of reality, remember that you have family, work and community. Take into account that work is a part of what is, not all that is.

7. Learn to say no.

Trust your intuition, do not accept jobs, projects or positions that you do not want. Do not feel compromised for having previously rejected a project or position.

8. Ask for help when you need it.

Important for their development and ability to work individually and as a team.

9. Work better and no more.

Try to carry out more efficiently the tasks assigned to you and promise to meet your schedule and do not accumulate jobs, much less take them home. Do what you consider most convenient but try as much as possible to do it because you want to, not because they force or pressure you.

10. Find meaning in your life and everything you do.

If you do not know what you want and what you do, your life has no meaning, you have to look inside yourself to make you happy, and then apply it in your daily life.

11. Do not strive to achieve perfection.

Do not obsess about jobs that are not as planned.

12. Evaluate yourself periodically.

Every time you can see how your labor market is and what companies would be interested in you.

Now, but, what happens if you are in a sectarian enterprise and you are not well, you already have some aspects described here that are part of your personal and work life. In this case you have no options or reasons to continue in the company where you are and I think you should take into consideration the following recommendations

1. Start with you, analyzing yourself and putting your definition of success.

You must take into account that you are a human being first of all, that you have emotions and feelings, and that you also have life projects. If the analysis has its definition of success and is not related to the company where it is, it is time to leave or resume the direction of his life.

2. Change employment.

Do your best to find a new job where you are comfortable and meet your expectations. Remember that the job you have is not the only job that exists and if it is the one you like, look for an equal job, but in another company.

3. Seek professional help.

You must be sick or you must have health problems, you may not notice it, but, you need to visit specialists, especially in these areas: psychology and general medicine. It is advisable to have a psychological treatment, to know how you are, how they can help you and what things depend on you and what does not. Do not go alone with your wife or close family member.

4. Expand your relationships.

If you when you were in school or in college, you had friends and colleagues with whom you entertained and shared because now you do not have or can not

have friends. Expand your ability to make and
improve your personal relationships, participate in
sporting events or attend camps and excursions.

5. Give meaning to your life.

Spend time with your family, go to the movies, to the
theater, make games and meetings with neighbors
and friends or plan visits or meetings with your
friends, you will see that you can take advantage of
that time to know how important it is and how much it
contributes to others outside. From his job.

6. Try to start your own business.

If you are an expert in your area, do not hesitate to
start your own business or to start a micro business,
you will be your own boss and most importantly, you

will set your rules and regulations, dedicate time to your family and work according to your convenience.

7. Get rid of old patterns.

Take the reins of your life, forget that you are the company or that the company is nothing without you, nothing is further from reality, believe it or not you are replaceable, if you leave it will put another in your place and dies while inside the company is worse because they will only tell their wife or husband "He was part of the family, but he is no longer with us". And not only that if they offered you a charge, or benefit or increase and they have not given it to you and you already fulfilled your part forget that they are going to give it, do not believe in false promises.

8. Look for your independence.

As previously stated, get rid of everything that ties you to the company, such as house, car, courtesy passes, use of laundry, use of gym, use of daycare, etc. Pay for the services you need and get what you can for your effort.

9. Prepare and educate yourself in your area.

The more studied and prepared the better for you as a person and as a professional, then you will have your doors open in any company.

10. Do other things.

Learn to perform other activities than the one you do, take courses in a trade or a topic that you like, thus broadening your work and leisure field.

I know that with the recommendations explained in this chapter, you will change your way of thinking, acting and living. You will take seriously that your independence and your inner being are more important than a company, organization or firm.

Chapter VII.

Punctual Recommendations.

You will surely wonder how do I avoid a sectarian enterprise next time? Well, although it does not create the answer to that question is already answered in the previous chapters, anyway it is advisable to take note of these specific points:

- The Ad: Remember that the ads are identical to the example shown here.

- The Interview: Take into account the points discussed here about the interview.

- <u>The Company</u>: There will be companies that you will not know how to identify until you are inside it. In this case, pay attention to the points discussed in this book regarding the company.

- <u>Preparing</u>: The more and better you are prepared, the easier it will be to identify a sectarian company.

- <u>Being Independent</u>: If you know how to differentiate what is and what you do, it will be difficult for you to fall into a sectarian enterprise.

- <u>Learning Different</u> Trades or Professions: Having more capacity and a large number of trades and / or professions, you will have a range of opportunities, difficult to see for a person with a single profession or trade.

- <u>Being Unique and Happy with what you do</u>: If you know what you do, like it and are happy, be sure it will not fall on sectarian businesses and if it falls you can leave quickly.

In addition to this I recommend you read my book "Stormy Jobs" since it sets out the characteristics of this type of employment and how to identify them, you will also find a series of recommendations to improve your quality of life.

Sectarian Companies   Ismael Bello

Final Notes.

As I have told you in almost the whole book, I would like to know your opinion and your answers to the questions asked in the book and that is why at the end of this section are my email addresses, so that you can send your answers, comments and suggestions regarding this topic.

Finally I just want to say something, we are all born free and nothing and nobody can take away that right, we can not allow a person, company or institution to manipulate us and take over our integrity, precisely, independence and integrity is what makes the Being unique human, because, is able to think and decide what I think best, suits or likes.

If you are part of a sectarian enterprise, I hope that this book has helped you and that it is not too late for you. If you are not, but you know someone who is or may be in a sectarian business, it is the moment that helps or advises you according to what is explained here. Personally I was in a sectarian enterprise and I know how to suffer and how to live within an organization of this type.

I suggest you read the book again, and focus on the points that have to do with you, seek advice and information from experts in the area and most importantly do not wait for tomorrow, start today, this is the best time to act .

Look at the past to correct, the future to project and the present to act, so if you meet or know someone who is in one of the situations named here do not wait any longer, start now!

I hope that this book has understood, understood and most importantly, that from now on you get the most out of it, for yourself, for your family, for your colleagues or for your friends.

Do not forget to send me your answers, suggestions and comments.

A hug.

Ismael Bello

Sectarian Companies   Ismael Bello

For suggestions and comments on this book use the following means:

E - Mail: ismael828@gmail.com

Twiter: @ismaelbello

Facebook: https://www.facebook.com/ismaelbello.527

Instagram: @ismaelbello1

Sectarian Companies   Ismael Bello

Bibliography

ARNOTT, Dave. The Cult of the Company. Editorial Paidos. Buenos Aires: 2002. P.P 272.

ASSENS, Jordi. Eggs With Bacon. Editorial Grupo Norma. Bogotá: 2008. P.P. 102

KJERULF, Alexander. The Happy Hour is from 9 to 5. Editorial Contentspanish. USA 2001. P.P. 213.

STRONG, José. Mobbing, Psychoterrorism at Work. Editorial Grupo Aran. Madrid: 2004. P.P. 79

NEWHOUSE, Robert. The Danger of the Sects. Editorial Edicomunicación. Madrid: 2000. P.P. 197

Dictionary of the Royal Spanish Academy 2018.

http://www.acosolaboral.net

http://www.universia.es

Sectarian Companies   Ismael Bello

About the Author.

Ismael Bello is a teacher, director of Corporación Tisem 2000 CA, broadcaster, radio producer, audiovisual director and writer. He is fond of sports, music and good food.

He has made different writings for different media among them: newspaper and radio. "Sectarian Companies" has been the book with which he began this path of writing, for everything that happened to him at work when he worked as an employee in a service company. He has written in other literary genres such as theater and narrative, books that will be available soon.

He has always liked freedom, so he thinks that this book is very important for you, both in the personal and professional field.

In the words of Ismael: "Do not let anyone control your life, do it from today and be free."

Other books by the same author:

"Stormy Jobs", How to identify them and how to get out of them.

"How to Make a Radio Program".

Sectarian Companies   Ismael Bello

Sectarian Companies   Ismael Bello

www.ingramcontent.com/pod-product-compliance
Lightning Source LLC
Chambersburg PA
CBHW031925170526
45157CB00008B/3049